W9-BKQ-559

Union Churches in North Carolina

During the

Eighteenth and Nineteenth Centuries

By

Bernard W. Cruse, Jr.

2001

Privately Published by Bernard W. Cruse, Jr.
146 Fryling Avenue, S.W.
Concord, North Carolina 28025-5741

Printed in the United States of America

First Edition, 2001

Library of Congress Card Number: 2001118080

ISBN 0-9712379-0-5

Table of Contents

Preface

In the beginning of the twenty-first century, it's time to take a look back nearly three hundred years to the eighteenth and nineteenth centuries and review what many people have forgotten and a lot of people never knew about the beginnings of the German Protestant Churches in North Carolina.

When our ancestors left their homeland and journeyed into the New World to seek not only means to make a living and live in peace, but religious freedom to worship in their true faith. When they arrived in the American colonies, they brought with them their bibles, hymnals, prayerbooks and their belief that their faith led to their salvation. Stymied at first by the few numbers in any one faith, they learned that they had kindred souls in a number of Protestant faiths, so it was only logical to join forces for worship, be they Lutheran, Reformed, Moravian, Episcopalian, Presbyterian and many others.

In the early years there were no resident ministers, so they relied, first, on the reading of services by certain elders and others and visits by itinerant ministers traveling through, although some of their credentials may have been questionable. Many baptisms, marriages, funerals and other services never saw the benefit of clergy because there was no clergy available.

When they began their schools and formal worship houses, people of two (or more) denominations combined forces and efforts and created what became Union Churches. This continued through the nineteenth century and some Union Churches even continued into the early twentieth century until a particular denomination was strong enough to branch out and build their own house of worship.

Here, collected from several sources, is the story. Please note that there may be spellings, verbiage and other inconsistences within quoted passages that have remained faithful to their origin rather than to be "square bracketed." Most of this volume may be called "cut and paste" for much of its context comes from previously published work. In the index, an attempt has been made to more completely identify persons identified only by a surname within the text.

Foreword

In a day such as our own, when the ecumenical spirit is alive in theological circles and beyond, it is encouraging to recognize the contribution of Bernard W. Cruse, Jr. to the history of the Reformed and Lutheran Churches in the southeastern United States.

Cruse serves on the History Committee of the North Carolina Lutheran Synod, transcribed the *Rothrock Diaries* and did extensive work on *All One Body: The Story of the North Carolina Lutheran Synod, 1803-1993* among other works. In his prior work as well as the current volume Cruse deserves credit for his careful study of the Reformed (United Church of Christ) and Lutheran Churches in the eighteenth and nineteenth centuries as well as their cooperation well into the twentieth century. Both churches were heavily influenced by the German language. Although both kept their historical identity, many times they met in common houses of worship and heard the same pastors who proclaimed the gospel message in familiar terms.

After moving to North America the German immigrants took the road south through the Shenandoah valley of Virginia into portions of North Carolina, South Carolina and Georgia. The early German churches which were formed in the new world, using the language of the majority of their parishioners, became centers of religious and social life. The sacraments were celebrated, children baptized, couples married and the dead buried in the language of the Fatherland. Often the grammar of German construction was different when used in the services of Lutheran and Reformed congregations. The Lord's Prayer was used by both of them, although there were minor differences in the language employed. Cruse points out these differences between the two versions. Lutherans began their rendition in the following manner:

Vater Unser, der du bist im himmel
Geheiliget werde Dein name
Dein Reich komme
Dein Wille geschehe wie im Himmel, also
Auch auf Erden

The Reformed people began:
Unser Vater in dem Himmel
Dein Name werde geheiliget
Dein Reich komme. Dein Will geische auf
Erden, wie im Himmel

The "Union Churches", consisting mainly of Lutheran and Reformed but sometimes occasional unions between Moravians and Episcopalians were attempted by Lutherans. As the American Revolution approached the Reformed people under the leadership of men like the Rev. Samuel Suther embraced the more radical ideas of the revolutionary fathers while the Lutherans maintained their loyalty to Great Britain.

Increasing numbers led the two groups to form their separate congregations although the union process lasted well into the twentieth century. An interesting account which illustrates the division of congregations is Grace Reformed Church near Salisbury. It is called "Lower Stone" and its beautiful stone walls with German inscriptions over the doors was an architectural achievement. German Lutherans who formed part of the congregation withdrew and formed Zion Lutheran Church nearby and it is called "Organ Church" because of the presence of a pipe organ in the building.

For Lutheran and Reformed descendants of those who brought their faith to the new world and guided its spiritual development through the ages, Cruse's volume offers an overview of the early union churches, their faith and the social fabric that influenced the early life of our nation. Those who do not stand in the German tradition will find it delightful reading in an area too long forgotten.

The Rev. Dr. Robert W. Delp
(Retired) Minister, United Church of Christ
803 Trail One
Burlington, NC 27215

December, 1999

UNION. In union there is strength. That philosophy insured the creation and lasting of the American republic known as the United States of America in the latter part of the eighteenth century. Fifty years earlier that same philosophy insured the creation and lasting of the mighty Lutheran and German Reformed (now a part of the United Church of Christ), Moravian, Presbyterian, Episcopal and other churches that have endured and will endure on into the twenty-first century and beyond in North Carolina. This work is intended to dwell on the Lutherans and German Reformeds who settled in the Piedmont section of North Carolina. There were (and are) a number of Lutheran-Episcopal unions in the eastern part of North Carolina who also allied for the same reasons, but we will not attempt to document them here.

When our forefathers were compelled to leave the mother country in the eighteenth century, it was mainly for religious reasons, but they absolutely did not leave their religion there. They brought with them their bibles, prayer books and religious tracts, but most important, their faith. Most of our immediate German ancestors entered the United States through the port of Philadelphia because of William Penn's efforts to colonize the New World for the benefit of the English crown beginning in 1707 (some as early as 1682)[1]. By the time our immigrant ancestors came, all the choice, large tracts of farm land in that area (Pennsylvania) had been taken. They were committed to live there and work to pay off their passage and other expenses to come to America, but as soon as they were able, they left Pennsylvania to seek lands they could obtain to farm and raise their families.

More or less in competition with William Penn, the Lords Proprietors had begun setting up a newer world in the Carolinas. Here was land that these new German immigrants could obtain to farm and raise their families. From the early 1740s through the Revolutionary War, thousands of them followed the Great Wagon

---

[1] WELKER, P13

Road down through Virginia into the Carolinas.

As soon as they could raise a roof over their heads and get crops started, they began thinking of the most important things in their society, church and schools. By the very nature of their initial colonization, population density was sparse. Most of the farms had a very minimum of one hundred acres; many were five hundred acres or more. Translated into population density, this meant that there were often no more than four or five farms in a given square mile; therefore a community of twenty or thirty families was spread out over several miles. This caused them to band together and put up some sort of shelter where they could worship and have school for their children.

Most of these immigrants were either Swiss or German. The Lutheran Church was founded in the sixteenth century by Martin Luther, and later John Calvin founded the German Reformed Church claiming that Martin Luther was not absolutely correct in some of his theologies. This work will not attempt to discuss the differences between the German Reformed and the Lutheran Church. Suffice to say that their religions were so alike that members of the two faiths felt very comfortable with one another. In 1943, in his book *Rhinelanders on the Yadkin* Carl Hammer wrote "There is also the story of how, in the days when German was still in general use, one man asked another: 'What is the real difference between the two denominations, anyway?' - 'Why,' said the other, 'it is all in the way they begin the Lord's Prayer: the one says 'Unser Vater', and the other 'Vater Unser'."[2]

Welker stated: "From the beginning of the German settlements in North Carolina, the Reformed and Lutherans were

---

[2] HAMMER, P62, SEE APPENDIX B

very closely allied, and nearly all their churches were union churches, where, on alternate Sabbaths, they worshiped, and this is still the case in a number of congregations [1908]. The members of these churches were also greatly intermarried, so that passing from one communion to the other never was a difficult question. Indeed, they did not make any account of the confessional differences, and really knew no difference. In a paper before the writer, when the two confessions agree to unite in the building of a house of worship, they give as a reason for such union that, 'Since we are both united in the principal doctrines of Christianity, we find no difference between us except in name.'"[3]

Therefore, it was very easy for these Germans to unite their efforts toward schooling and religious worship and create a larger, stronger entity than either could achieve by themselves.

"In each settlement, without fail, was a 'house of worship.' Usually congregations organized themselves into union churches, composed of Lutherans and Reformed neighbors, and others who chose to become a part of the fellowship. These were ministered to by available preachers, usually of the Reformed or Lutheran faiths, and managed by officers elected by the cooperating congregations. As these communities expanded and more ministers became available, the desire for denominational organizations and separate churches became keener. One by one union churches disappeared. At the present time [1968] only one union church appears on the roll of the Southern Synod, that being Salem Church, Lincoln County."[4]

The original German Reformed Church, (now a part of the

---

[3] WELKER, PP16-17

[4] PEELER P5

United Church of Christ), was one of the earliest to be established in Virginia, South Carolina, and the Piedmont section of North Carolina. The historical records of the churches and schools which it established prove it was here at an early date.[5]

The authentic records connected with the beginnings and final consummation of the establishment of the first Reformed congregation in Virginia constitute one of the most interesting chapters in the history of the Reformed Church in the United States (known as the German Reformed Church previously to World War I), and it is doubtful if the beneficent influence radiating from any one of the early congregations can favorably compare with that which emanated from it, and enriched the spiritual and material well-being of many sections of our great country.

". . . upon their arrival in 1714, were settled by Governor Spotswood on the Rapidan River in the northern corner of the present Orange County [VA]. Here they built their log cottages and fortified their small villages with palisades and a block house, which was also used as a place of worship. The village was named Germanna in honor of the Fatherland, and the 'Good Queen Ann' of England."[6]

"The first German settlement in what is now North Carolina was established by two Swiss, Louis Michel and Baron Christopher de Graffenried, who hoped to make their fortune by creating a colony in Carolina. As in other colonizing attempts, they sent out persons to recruit prospective settlers for the colony. Such recruiters, or "newlanders", were not above making extravagant claims because their compensation was based on the number of

---

[5] BEAR CREEK, P1

[6] BEAR CREEK, P13

settlers they recruited. Naturally, those responsible for the recruiting went to territories flooded with refugees from Europe's incessant warfare and religious strife. Thus, the Palatines were frequently the objects of recruiting efforts.

"There was also some selective recruiting of persons with particular talents. De Graffenried hoped that the land between the Neuse and the Cape Fear rivers he had been awarded by the Lords Proprietors of Carolina would contain deposits of valuable ores and minerals. Therefore, he recruited a number of German iron workers from Nassau-Seigen to send to Carolina. But in 1714, de Graffenried released the twelve families to the Lieutenant-Governor of Virginia, Alexander Spotswood, who had discovered iron deposits on his lands on the Rappahannock. These immigrant iron workers at Germanna, who later established a new community at Germantown in Fauquier County, created the oldest German Reformed congregation in America."[7]

A shaft of stone honoring the 1714 immigrants, erected temporarily on Route 3, was relocated at private expense at this permanent site in Seigen Forest. it bears this inscription:

SITE OF THE FIRST
GERMAN REFORMED CHURCH

HERE AT GERMANNA 1714 THE FIRST PERMANENT
GERMAN REFORMED CONGREGATION IN AMERICA
LOCATED WITH THEIR PASTOR REV. HENRY
HAEGER. THEY WERE A FAMILY OF THIRTEEN
FAMILIES FROM NASSAU-SEIGEN, GERMANY. WHO
WERE WELCOMED TO VIRGINIA BY GOVERNOR
SPOTSWOOD AND WHO WERE SETTLED HERE TO

[7] BOST AND NORRIS, P4

DEVELOP HIS IRON INDUSTRY AND TO PROTECT
THIS AREA OF THE FRONTIER. THEY FOUNDED
GERMANTOWN, FAUQUIER COUNTY, AND MOVED
THERE ABOUT 1720.

HEADS OF THE IMMIGRANT FAMILIES

Melcherd Brumbach	John Hoffman
John Camper (Kemper)	Jacob Holtzeclaw
John Coontz (Coons)	John Joseph Martin
Herman Fishback	John Jacob Rector
John Fishback	John Spillman
Peter Hitt (?)	Dillman Weaver

ERECTED 1953 BY THE
EVANGELICAL AND REFORMED CHURCH. . .

This is irrefutable evidence that German Reformed families
were settled in Virginia by 1714–and suggests the possibility that
they may have been coming in North Carolina long before the
organization date of the Dutch Buffalo Creek Church.

"As further evidence that the Reformed and Lutheran folk of
Germany were closely related in their settlement and beginnings in
this country, and in their church life, there is also a marker in the
Germanna area with this inscription:

"THIS MARKER HONORS
THE MEMORY OF THE SECOND
GERMANNA COLONY. 1717
TWENTY GERMAN FAMILIES FROM THE UPPER
RHINE VALLEY, MOSTLY LUTHERANS, SETTLED
NEAR THIS SITE IN 1717 AND WERE PROMPTLY

FOLLOWED BY OTHERS, SOME OF THEM INDEBTED TO GOVERNOR SPOTSWOOD FOR MONEY HE HAD ADVANCED FOR THEIR PASSAGE, DISCHARGED THE DEBT BY ASSISTING IN THE OPERATION OF HIS IRON MINES. ABOUT 1725 THEY REMOVED FARTHER UP TO LANDS ACQUIRED BY GRANT IN THE ROBINSON RIVER SECTION OF MADISON COUNTY. HERE NEAR WHITE OAK RUN IN 1740 THEY BUILT HEBRON LUTHERAN CHURCH WHICH STILL STANDS A MONUMENT TO THEIR DEVOTION AND CHRISTIAN CHARACTER

"HEADS OF FAMILIES

BALTHASER BLANKENBAKER	MICHAEL KAIFER
MATTHIAS BLANKENBAKER	ANDREW KERKER
NICHOLAS BLANKENBAKER	GEORGE MOYER
JOHN BROYLES	JOHN MOTZ
JOHN CARPENTER (1721)	GEORGE SHEIBLE
WILLIAM CARPENTER (1721)	MATTHEW SMITH
MICHAEL CLORE	MICHAEL SMITH
MICHAEL COOK	HENRY SNYDER
ZEKECHIAS FLESHMAN	GEORGE UTZ
JOHN HARNSBERGER	NICHOLAS YAGER
MICHAEL HOLT	CHRISTOPHER ZIMMERMAN

"ERECTED BY JAMES CARLTON CLORE IN HONOR OF HIS PARENTS MAY FRANCES YOWELL AND JAMES CLEVELAND CLORE, DESCENDANTS OF MICHAEL CLORE "ERECTED IN 1961"[8]

"These historical references reveal again the very close relationship existing between the Reformed and the Lutheran

---

[8] BEAR CREEK, PP15-16

people in the early days in America. For approximately a quarter of a century the Lutherans had no pastors of their own faith, at least in Virginia and North Carolina. Their people shared in the ministry of the Reformed pastors and teachers. Members of these two churches were among the very first to settle in that area of Virginia and to establish churches.

"GERMAN REFORMED CHURCHES ARE IN SOUTH CAROLINA

"The German Reformed Church had twenty to thirty congregations very early in the settling of the State of South Carolina.

"We read of Reformed and Lutheran people in South Carolina in the early 1700s. 'In the year 1737 a German colony, called Saxe-Gotha, was settled along the upper course of the Congaree River, near the junction of the Broad and Saluda rivers, it was settled largely by the Swiss. As the Lutheran pastors kept up friendly relations with their Reformed neighbors, there are numerous important references to the Reformed pastors and congregations in South Carolina and Georgia . . . In 1741 the news of the erection of the new Township of Saxe-Gotha reached the Lutheran pastors at Ebenezer. They write, under date of December 2, 1741:

"'We had heard nothing before of Saxe-Gotha in America, but we have just received intelligence that such a town is laid out in South Carolina, 100 English miles (or 25 German miles) from Charles-Town, on the road which passes through Orangeburg, and is settled with German people. Doubtless the majority of them are Reformed people, because they have a Reformed minister among them, with whose character we are not yet acquainted.' This Reformed minister was the Rev. Christian Theus'. He was ordained in 1739, as we have stated 'From 1739 he officiated as minister among the German Reformed settlers of South Carolina,' and the Lutherans.

"Mr. Theus was present at a meeting in 1789. As this is the last time that his name is mentioned, it is assumed that he died shortly thereafter.

"Mr. Theus had a fine education, and his learning and piety were highly spoken of. Rev. Christian Theus was a great and good man, and was the first minister among the Swiss and Germans of Carolina. If there had been formed a 'Coetus', covering the Carolinas and Georgia, in those early years, the Reformed Church would now have a different story to write of its work and people in the South. A few faithful men, such as Theus, Froelich, Martin, Dupert, Suther, Penager, Zubly, Schneider, Bithaln, Loretz, stood alone for years and did their work well. But in South Carolina and Georgia they had no successors. But the labors of Mr. Theus were not in vain. He fostered the weak German churches in North Carolina and held them together until permanent ministers came and located there. The Classis of North Carolina, does well, even at this late date, to pay tribute to Rev. Christian Theus, whose labors in those early years prepared the way for future success."[9]

"The Germans in North Carolina did not have the clear, religious patrimony of the Salzburgers whose immigration to the New World was conspicuously related to their devotion to the evangelical faith. Nevertheless, they have been described as "fervently religious.""

"Later descendants of these early settlers inherited German Bibles, hymnals and devotional works like *True Christianity* by John [Johann Gottfried] Arndt. Devout they were, but they were divided in their religious loyalties. The Moravians, coming as a conscious and well-planned expansion of a base of operations in Pennsylvania, concentrated their settlements near Salem which early emerged as the center of Moravian operations in the South.

"Other German settlers, whether choosing to establish

---

[9] BEAR CREEK, PP17-18

themselves in the valley of Virginia, the Dutch Fork of South Carolina or Piedmont North Carolina, were, denominationally speaking, usually a mixture of German Reformed and Lutherans. For a number of decades, they jointly supported a teacher to instruct their children, shared in common places of worship and selected their hymns of praise to God from the same hymnal. Unlike the Salzburgers in Georgia and the Moravians at Salem, these Reformed and Lutheran settlers in the interior of Virginia and the Carolinas did not bring clergy with them when they left Pennsylvania to move south. While the Reformed often seemed more efficient than their Lutheran neighbors in securing the service of an ordained pastor, there was such an acute and endemic shortage of clergy that both Lutheran and Reformed lay persons gratefully accepted the ministrations of an ordained pastor of either tradition.

"But while almost always devoid of pastoral leadership, these settlers early began to make provision for their own spiritual nurture and that of their families. Devout lay persons were gathering their relatives and German-speaking neighbors for worship in at least informal congregations as early as 1745, even though for many years the best they could expect by way of worship leadership was the equivalent of a lay reader, an occasional visit from a Moravian missionary, or the services of some wandering German whose pastoral credentials might not withstand close scrutiny. It seems probable that the congregations that later became known as Friedens, Gibsonville, St. John's and Zion (Organ), Salisbury; and St. John's, Concord, were already functioning congregations by 1750. In the next two decades ; St. Paul's, Alamance; Reformation, Mocksville; Philadelphia, Dallas; Daniel's, Lincolnton; St. Paul's, Newton; Pilgrim, Lexington; and Cold Water, Concord, emerged as congregations.

"Here in the gathered Christian community, the German settlers, weighted down with the knowledge that their eyes would never again behold the Fatherland, and, short of eternity, would never again see friends and relatives left behind in Germany, could at least find spiritual sustenance and nurture proffered in their native tongue. The bonds of fellowship forged by a common faith expressed in a common language carried over into the daily living of the German settlers, and those who, from the outside, observed their ready willingness to support one another were generous in their praise of the personal qualities that characterized most of the German settlers.

"The fact that, outside the Moravian settlement, none of the congregations created by German settlers in Piedmont North Carolina in the 1740s and 1750s regularly enjoyed in its early years the services of a resident pastor, either Lutheran or Reformed, does not mean that pastors were never present in these congregations. Reformation, Mocksville, is a case in point. Established as Heidelberg Evangelical Lutheran Church, but popularly known as the Dutchman's Creek church, this congregation was functioning as early as 1766 and quite possibly went back to the beginning of that decade and the founding of the settlement. George Soelle, a Dane who was ordained as a Lutheran in his native land and entered the Unity of the Brethren in 1748, came to the American colonies in 1753. In 1770, he moved with several families to the Carolina settlement called Wachovia. During the years 1771-73, he conducted numerous missionary tours among Germans in Piedmont North Carolina."[10]

Just how long the Heidleberg Reformed congregation at Dutchman's Creek existed or when it disbanded is not known. The

---

[10] BOST AND NORRIS, PP22-23

Lutheran congregation continued until 1925. In 1815, the congregation, possibly just Lutheran, relocated a mile or so away, then in 1873 was again relocated, reorganized and named "Reformation" but was popularly known as Cherry Hill.[11]

"By the middle 1740s Lutherans and Reformed were worshiping together in Rowan County and in that part of Mecklenburg County that fifty years later (1792) became Cabarrus County. Exact dates are not available for written records were not deemed necessary at that time, but Hickory Church in eastern Rowan County was built sometime around 1754 or 1755.[12] The combined Lutheran and Reformed congregation had worshiped together for something like ten years before building that formal edifice. They continued to worship together for at least another forty years after that when the Lutherans built their Zion Lutheran Church and the Reformed built their Grace Reformed Church some distance west of the original location. One of Zion's members, John Stirewalt, built and installed in the Lutheran church the first pipe organ in the state,[13] so Zion became known thereafter as "Organ" Church. Both buildings were beautiful large stone works, and because of its geographical location, Grace became known as "Lowerstone" Church. As of this writing in 2001, Grace Lowerstone is still worshiping in their magnificent stone building, but Organ built a modern larger building more than twenty years ago.

About the same time, not too far away, on the banks of Bear Creek in the extreme western part of Stanly County Lutherans and

---

[11] PEELER, P450

[12] WELKER, P193

[13] HAMMER, P35

Reformeds united to form what was first referred to as "Barren Creek" Church.[14] By 1747 some of the Lutherans at Bear Creek left to form St. John's Lutheran Church in a part of Mecklenburg County that later became Cabarrus County. Welker wrote: "The Reformed and Lutherans worshiped in the same church harmoniously for many years, electing the same officers, and sometimes supporting the same pastor. But in course of time it became evident that a division would be better, and this was effected August 16, 1875. The Reformed congregation retained the church lands, consisting of 110 acres, and the old church, while the Lutherans secured a new site and built about two miles east. Many Lutherans united with the Reformed Church."[15] While the Reformeds kept the name of Bethel (Bear Creek) Church, the new Lutheran congregation took the name New Bethel Evangelical Lutheran Church.

In the middle 1750s Frieden's (Schumaker's) Church in Gibsonville and Richland's Church in Liberty were organized. Shiloh Church in Forsyth County was organized about this same time, a Lutheran-Moravian Union. In 1855 Savitz's Church was established in Rowan County, in 1857 Pilgrim's (Leonard's) Church started in Davidson County and in 1859 St. Paul's began their worship in Catawba County.

"Frieden's Church is located two miles north from Gibsonville, in Guilford County, N.C. This is one of the oldest Lutheran churches in North Carolina. Although we do not know just when it was organized, yet we do know that it was prior to the Revolutionary War. During that war there was a man by the name of Schumaker lived a few hundred yards from the church. This man

---

[14] WELKER, P215

[15] WELKER, P218

was a 'Tory,' and, upon a certain occasion, refused to give a drink of water to a wounded soldier. This so infuriated his companions that they took the man Schumaker to the church, made him stand on the door-steps, and shot him there. He is buried in the old graveyard. From this circumstance the church was often called 'Schumaker's Church.' Originally the congregation was composed of Lutherans and German Reformed, who had together come from Pennsylvania. About the year 1855 they separated, and it has since been wholly Lutheran."[16]

"The northeast corner of Randolph County was peopled, as Guilford, by Germans from Pennsylvania between the years 1750 and 1760. At an early day the Reformed and Lutherans built a union church, still known as 'Richlands.' Richland Church is located in Randolph County, four miles north from Liberty. Owing perhaps to the same causes that made the separation in the "Low" Church, the Reformed people soon moved to a house of their own, built near the village of Liberty, on the road that led from Guilford Court House Cross Creek, or Fayetteville. According to the best information, the congregation was organized about the year 1791, under the leadership of Rev. Christian Eberhardt Bernhardt, who came to this vicinity in 1789. The congregation was then composed of Lutherans and German Reformed, and continued thus until about the year 1802, when it became wholly Lutheran."[17]

"Barton's (Richland's) was located in the northeast corner of Randolph County, about one mile north of the town of Liberty. The church was started about 1776 or soon thereafter, by people of the Reformed and Lutheran faiths. It was first called Barton's Meeting House.

---

[16] BERNHEIM AND COX, P108

[17] WELKER, P135; BERNHEIM AND COX, P124

"After a few years the Reformed and Lutherans separated. The Reformed congregation moved to a house of their own, nearer to the town of Liberty...

"...After that time, it was allowed to go down finally disappearing from the roll of congregations [of the Reformed Church]. There are no records providing further details."[18]

"Shiloh Church is located twelve miles west from Winston, N. C., in Forsyth County, and constituted a part of the Forsyth Mission. It is unknown when the congregation was first organized, but there are traditions reaching back to a very early date. It is supposed to have been a union congregation with the Moravians, as some of the pastors of that church preached there. It is now entirely Lutheran, but when the separation was effected is not known."[19]

"...on the west side of Muddy Creek, a meetinghouse was built in 1782, by a German Lutheran and Reformed congregation, wherein, since the year 1797, divine service is held by some of the ministers of the Brethren's (Moravian) church, every fourth Sunday, in the German language."[20]

"Mt. Zion Reformed Church is located in Rowan County a mile south of the present town of China Grove. It is on the north side of the Southern Railway and the large brick church and the neatly kept cemetery present a fine appearance as viewed from passing trains. This church was originally known as 'Savitz's,' in

---

[18] PEELER, P442

[19] BERNHEIM AND COX, PP149-150

[20] PEELER, P453

some later records corrupted into 'Savage's,' but the real name from the first is supposed to have been Mt. Zion. The date of its origin is unknown. German settlers came to this community as early as 1745 and earlier. They were members of the Reformed and Lutheran Churches. The first resident pastor was Rev. Samuel Suther, who lived near the old 'Coldwater Church.' The members who organized Savitz's Church may have been at first connected with Coldwater Church, as that seems to be the older of the two. But in the absence of positive records dates cannot be fixed. It is possible that 'Savitz's Church' was organized prior to the coming of Martin and Dupert to this German settlement of North Carolina. The following tradition may refer to a date as early as 1755. This traditional history comes down from a man by the name of Allen Rose, a school teacher who taught in the school-house at the old Savitz's Church. The story was given to Allen Rose by an old Mr. Shuping, and by Mr. Rose was given to his son Calvin Rose. This tradition says that the church was originally to be located two or two and a half miles west of the present site, on a farm now owned by Joseph Sechler. The logs had all been cut and placed on the grounds. The day for the raising of the walls was appointed, and all the people gathered and began work in good earnest. But after the foundation was laid and the first logs placed, one of the builders became offended at a remark made by another. This brought on a quarrel in which a large majority of those present took part. In the midst of the disturbance a peacefully disposed gentleman threw down his axe and declared: 'I do not propose to be a party in the erection of a house for Almighty God that has been begun in bitter strife.' Others followed his example, and soon the work came to an end. Nothing more was ever done at this point, and the timbers were allowed to go to decay. But two of the workers started home, traveling east. They were anxious to have a house of worship for themselves and their German brethren. Reaching the point where they must separate, they sat down to eat their dinner. Naturally their conversation was about the distressing affair of the morning. As they ate their dinner, one of the gentlemen remarked: 'This spot would be a desirable location for a church.' The other agreed that it would, provided water could be found near by. They then started out in search for water, and to their great joy found a spring conveniently near. This place was selected, and a little later a log church was built. It is the site of the present Mt. Zion Church. The first church was a small building, afterwards displaced by a larger one painted red. A half-witted man in the community conceived the idea that red was Satan's emblem, and he deliberately set fire to the building as he said in order to burn the devil. Another church was soon built on the same foundation. This church was occupied by the Reformed and Lutherans jointly until 1836. In that year the Lutherans withdrew and built a church of their own a few hundred yards away. The Reformed congregation continued to occupy the old church for a few years and then built a brick church on a lot of their own. This was in the year 1844."[21]

"Settling in that portion of Mecklenburg County that became Cabarrus, [Rev. Samuel] Suther based his ministry in the Cold Water, Grace (Lower Stone) and Dutch Buffalo Creek congregations, just east of present-day Concord, His was, however, a ministry that stretched from Mecklenburg County in the west to Orange County in the east, with ministry documented at Pilgrim near present-day Lexington as well as Low's, Liberty. In October 1771, Suther responded to a call to serve Brick Church in Guilford County. From that more easterly base of operations, he also continued to provide the Reformed and Lutheran Christians in Alamance, Davidson, Rowan, Cabarrus and Stanly Counties with occasional visits.

---

[21] WELKER, PP210-212

"The decision of Suther to relocate in Guilford County forced the German settlers on Second Creek in southeastern Rowan County to confront several realities. Although Suther had been living in the area for over three years, the folk had grown to appreciate having a settled, German-speaking pastor in their midst. No doubt Suther would visit them from time to time, just as he would continue his occasional visits to Germans in the other counties. But the Germans in Rowan no longer had nearby an ordained pastor who spoke German when a funeral was to be conducted, a baby baptized, or a new Christian home established through Holy Matrimony. Such matters had to wait for months until Suther, a Moravian missionary, or a Reformed pastor from South Carolina, happened to come by. Older persons, in particular, were concerned that, should death claim them, they might be months in their grave before a real pastor came along to say a prayer over their final resting place."[22]

In 1820, there was a split in the North Carolina Lutheran Synod which resulted in the creation of a new synod, called the Tennessee Synod. At that time, Lutherans worshiping at the above Mt. Zion and Savitz's, otherwise called Lutheran Chapel, split into two groups, the original staying with the North Carolina Lutheran Synod under the name of Lutheran Chapel and the new group organizing a new church, Mt. Moriah, affiliated with the Tennessee Synod. Thus, there were now three congregations worshiping on the same premises. Mt. Moriah later acquired land some distance to the southwest and built their own church building.

"Again, the Colonial Records indicate that German settlers were in this area in considerable numbers in the 1740s. 'The Mount Zion Church is about ten miles south of Salisbury, on the

---

[22] BOST AND NORRIS, P25

line of the North Carolina Railroad, near China Grove station. This was, in its foundation, known as 'Savitz' Church', which was a union church, the joint property of the Reformed and Lutheran people. When the church was organized, and by whom, we have no records to show. No doubt a place of worship was established here long before a regular minister was attainable, and an organization followed in the time of Suther or Loretz about 1760. Already in 1745-1750 all this region was peopled by the flood of immigration from Pennsylvania, as was that on Dutch Buffalo and Second Creeks.[23]

"The last sentence indicates that arrivals had been numerous in preceding years, and shows that our German ancestors were very early in coming into the Piedmont area of North Carolina for their permanent homes."[24]

"In 1799 the German Lutherans in China Grove joined with the German Reformed Christians to build a permanent house of worship. About four acres of land was purchased from George Savitz for the sum of five pounds and the deed was made to 'Conrad Sloop, Jacob Bostian, Adam Correll and Jacob Correll (all of the County and State aforesaid), Elders and Trustees for the United German Congregation of Presbyterians and Lutherans (sic) in Rowan County near George Savitz' of the other part'. A log building was built on the site and was painted red. A man in the community who was mentally disturbed considered red to be the color of the devil, and had wanted the Church painted blue, and when the building was painted red, he burned it down. The leaders of the congregation decided to rebuild the log structure and again, it was painted red.

---

[23] COLONIAL RECORDS, VOL. VIII P748 (QUOTED IN BEAR CREEK)

[24] BEAR CREEK, PP210-212

"The red log church building was often called 'Savitz Church' and the building served separate congregations of Lutherans and German Reformed Christians. The tie of common language in a country populated by English and English-speaking Scotch-Irish was strong, and the two congregations shared the facility for over thirty years. But while it is likely that many members of each congregation came to worship whenever a German service was held, the congregations shared only a building and a sense of Christian fellowship. Each congregation called and supported a pastor trained and ordained according to its tradition.

"While family ties with German Reformed Christians were being strengthened, the condition of Lutheranism in North Carolina was perilous. Only Arends and Storch remained of the German missionaries. They were helped by Robert Miller, an Episcopal Minister licensed by the Methodists, who had been ordained by the Lutherans in 1794 since there was no Episcopal Diocese in North Carolina; and by Paul Henkel, who was born in Rowan (now Davie) County and was licensed by the Ministerium of Pennsylvania in 1783 with annual renewal until his ordination in 1792. From his home in New Market, Virginia, Paul Henkel was a traveling preacher in North Carolina. In 1803, these four pastors met to organize the 'Synod of the Lutheran and Protestant Episcopal Church' (so-named to include Miller who had family ties elsewhere). Despite the official title, the Synod considered itself Lutheran. The charter of the North Carolina Lutheran Synod was signed by the four pastors and fourteen laymen, including Conrad Schlup (Sloop) of the Church at Irish Settlement.

"Pastor Storch served the congregation until 1820, and during those years, family ties remained strong. The congregation enjoyed a relationship with other German-speaking Christians through a shared worship facility, and through the newly organized

Synod which also had relationships with Moravians in Salem and with German Reformeds."[25]

"The German immigration into this section of North Carolina was at high tide from 1745 to 1755. These people came to North Carolina and took up great tracts of land in the most desirable sections of the State. The Germans were members either of the Reformed or Lutheran or Moravian Church. Being accustomed to regular services at home, they naturally were zealous to enjoy the same privileges in this country. But there was one great difficulty in the way of this, viz., the lack of ministers. The best that could be done was to appoint the older men and others of marked piety to conduct services of prayer and read printed sermons. Sometimes the school masters were appointed to conduct the meetings; but school teachers were almost as scarce as ministers. The Abbott's Creek section attracted quite a number of settlers within the period above designated. Among these were Jacob Hege and his sons George and Henry; Peter Spengler, Valentine Leonard and his brother Peter; Henry Shoaf, Jacob Berrier, Philip Sauer (Sowers), Christopher and George Sprecher, Adam Hedrick, Peter Meyer (Meyers) Adam Conrad, Jacob Byerly and George Clodfelter. Most of these men were from the Palatinate in Germany and were members of the Reformed Church, as were their children after them.

"In the year 1753 or 1754 Jacob Berrier and two or three companions were one day riding through the country between the Yadkin River and Abbott's Creek. There were then Indians in this section of North Carolina. Mr. Berrier and his companions had visited several settlers on the lands between and on the waters of these two streams. These people were neighbors, though they lived in some cases many miles apart. About three-quarters of a

---

[25] LUTHERAN CHAPEL, P4

mile west of Abbott's Creek these gentlemen came to a beautiful spot in a grove of oak, hickory and sugar-maple trees, where was also a spring of sparkling water bubbling up. Here they paused and Jacob Berrier said to his companions: *'Gott hat diese Stelle zur verehrung sines Namens gesehaffen; hier mussen wir ein Versammlungshaus haben.'* (God fashioned this place for a house of worship; here we must have a meeting-house.) This spot was near the home of Valentine Leonard, who came to North Carolina from Germany in 1746 and took up several tracts of the Lord Granville and Henry McCulloh lands on both sides of what was then called 'Mill Creek,' but afterwards and to this day called 'Leonard's Creek' after his name. Valentine Leonard was born at Katzenbach in the Palatinate, Germany, October 13, 1718. His parents were Martin and Anna Barbara Leonard, who were married November 11, 1704, by Rev. Carl Gervinus, pastor of the Reformed Church at Katzenbach from 1691 to 1710. Valentine Leonard was baptized October 23, 1718, in the Reformed Church at Katzenbach by the Rev. Gotthard Steitz, the pastor. He was confirmed a full member of the same church at Easter, 1733, by Rev. Henry Julius Wagner, pastor of the Katzenbach Reformed Church from 1719 to 1763. To Valentine Leonard and his wife Elizabeth were born eight children: Barbara, Valentine, Michael, Peter, Catharine, Elizabeth, Philip and Jacob. Barbara married Henry Hege, a son of Jacob Hege (both named above), and a brother of George Hege. Elizabeth married George Clodfelter. Valentine Leonard and his wife Elizabeth, his five sons and their wives, and his three daughters and sons-in-law were all members of the Reformed Church near his home, the church built on the spot pointed out by Jacob Berrier and afterwards known for many years as 'Leonard's Church,' from the fact that the church was near Valentine Leonard's house and also from the fact that he and his family constituted a large part of the membership in the early days of its history.

"Valentine Leonard, the pioneer, was a patriot in those stirring times preceding and during the American Revolution, as were also many of his neighbors. The pastor of the Reformed congregation at Pilgrim Church during these years was Rev. Samuel Suther, who served from 1768 to 1786. His pastorate covered the years of that stormy period, and being himself an intense patriot he naturally influenced his parishioners in that direction. Valentine Leonard and his sons fought through that struggle; the last battle in which they fought was that of Guilford Court House, March 15, 1781, after which they returned home. Near the close of the war, on the second day of November, 1781, a band of Tories came to Valentine Leonard's house and attempted to murder him, and in fact left him for dead. He died from his wounds November 13th, a martyr to his country He was buried in the grave-yard close by the church of which he was a faithful member and which before and since bore his name.

"The site of the church was selected in that interesting way by Jacob Berrier at that early date. Jacob Berrier was the father of John Martin and David Berrier, some of whose descendants are still citizens of the same community. There was no house of worship built until several years later. A brush arbor was put up on the spot, under which services were conducted occasionally by some of the older men. In these meetings many prayers were made to God earnestly asking for a minister. The spot selected was on an unoccupied tract of land lying between the lands of Philip Sauer (Sowers) on the north and Valentine Leonard on the south. Philip Sauer came to North Carolina in 1753 and took up a tract of land north of the present location of the church. Soon afterwards he married. The first baptismal entry in the record of the Reformed congregation at this place is that of his first-born child, Anna Catharine Sauer, the date of whose birth was April 27, 1757, and whose baptism was evidently not long afterwards. This child was the daughter of Philip Sauer and wife. The name of the officiating clergyman is not given. It is probable that Rev. Christian Theus, who lived in the forks of the Broad and Saluda Rivers in South

Carolina, baptized this child. He preached regularly in the upper part of South Carolina from 1739 to 1775 and also visited the German settlements in North Carolina and held services for the scattered Reformed people. He was the first Reformed preacher in this section of the country. Or it may be that the child was not baptized until 1759, when the Rev. Mr. Martin, a Swiss Reformed minister, preached regularly to the Reformed people on the waters of Abbott's Creek and the Yadkin River, as well as elsewhere in this section of the State. This baptismal record is an interesting book. There are thirty-six names of heads of families in the early records, though some of them had no children. The writing is in German and shows different hands. There are 179 baptisms from 1757 to 1798. Of these 179 baptisms, 145 are recorded prior to the year 1787, and 33 are recorded prior to 1772. The names of the god-parents (*Taufzeugen* in German), the persons who presented themselves with the parents at the altar in the baptism at the request of the parents, are given in nearly all the records.

"The first records of Pilgrim Reformed Church are incomplete. The oldest book in the possession of the congregation is this record of infant baptisms dating from 1757.

"The first church, which was built within the period 1757-1764, was a substantial log structure built on land claimed by McCulloh, though a tract of fifty acres lying between the lands of Philip Sauer and Valentine Leonard was laid off as church property. The official grant was made October 8, 1783, to the 'Elders in trust for the Dutch Congregation.' The first recorded name of the church is the 'Dutch Congregation' as given in this official paper; but the real name seems to have been 'Pilgrim Church,' or 'The Church of the Pilgrims.' It was called in the official records the 'Dutch Congregation' because it was the church located in the community known as the 'Dutch settlement on Abbott's Creek.' It was the only church, when it was organized, in that part of Rowan County east of the Yadkin River.

In the year 1787 the Lutherans came in as co-tenants, and from that time on had the use of the church and the lands. There is no record as to the terms on which they were admitted. For thirty-four years the two denominations worshiped in the same church. In 1821 the Lutherans split, and the two congregations of that denomination were allowed by the Reformed to use the property along with themselves until the spring of the year 1903, when the Reformed congregation, to gain absolute title to the entire property, paid to the two parties of Lutherans the handsome sum of $3,100.00 and received from them a quit-claim."[26]

"St. Paul's Church is located in Catawba County one and a half miles west of Newton, and is the oldest church by a number of years on the western border of that numerous German settlement in North Carolina in the counties of Alamance, Guilford, Randolph, Davidson, Rowan, Cabarrus, Stanley [sic], Iredell, Lincoln, Catawba and some others. These Germans, Lutherans and Reformed, began to migrate from Pennsylvania about 1745, because land in that State east of the Alleghenies was mostly taken up, but was plentiful, cheap and fertile in Western North Carolina. The exact date of the founding of St. Paul's is not known, but it is nearly co-eval with the beginning of the settlement. It is known that a Swiss minister by the name of Martin preached here in 1759, and doubtless the venerable and godly Theus preached here still earlier.

"St. Paul's was a union church from the beginning. The Reformed and Lutheran settlers for the most part built union churches, and worshiped and lived on terms of delightful harmony. Eleven acres were donated by Paul Anthony. The deed specifies that it was for a church and a school-house. Religion and education went together in those days. The school-master, in the

---

[26] WELKER, PP156-164

absence of the minister, often conducted services in the church, buried the dead and sometimes baptized the children."[27]

"St. Paul's Reformed Church, Startown, is rooted in the Old St. Paul's Church located two miles west of Newton, in the South Fork section of Catawba County. The latter place appears to have been some sort of focal point in 1702, perhaps earlier. For in the church cemetery is a grave stone bearing that date, and on it is inscribed 'Here lies in peace our beloved Abraham Mauser. He was old.' The area around the church was sparsely settled in 1712. Tradition relates that, 'As early as 1733...there was a crude, one-story log cabin between two white pines that was used for worship.' The old log cabin was struck by lightning, and burned to the ground. Later a new building was erected across the road in 1757."[28]

"St. Paul's Church is located in Catawba County, at Startown, two miles southwest of Newton. The original location of this church is two miles directly west of Newton where the St. Paul's of the American Lutheran Church is located.

"St. Paul's Church at Startown is a continuation of the old St. Paul's Church, which was organized about 1768 or 1770. A division arose in that church in 1845 when a part of the congregation withdrew from the Tennessee Synod and later unified with the Ohio Synod, now the American Lutheran Church. But a large group remained faithful to the Tennessee Synod. This group of the Tennessee Synod continued to worship in the old St. Paul's building until 1905 when, under the leadership of Rev. F. K. Roof, a lot was secured and a new frame church was built at Startown.

---

[27] WELKER, PP243-244

[28] PEELER, P403

Hence, we deem it historically correct to say that St. Paul's Church at Startown was first organized at the old location about 1768 0r 1770.

"The first building at the old place was a small log structure. But in 1808 a new church was built. This too was a log house, which was weatherboarded and ceiled. It is still used by the American Lutheran Congregation.

St. Paul's house of worship at Startown was built in 1905. It was destroyed by fire November 26, 1922, while Rev. W. J. Boger, D.D., was pastor. The following year a brick building was erected with a full basement and Sunday School rooms, and the first service was held on December 24, 1923."[29]

By 1759 at least eight Union Churches had come into existence and only two purely Lutheran churches. The Lutheran churches were the above named St. John's in Cabarrus County and another St. John's, this one in Salisbury in Rowan County. As far as evidenced by writings of Welker and his committee, Gottfried Dellman Bernheim and, again, Bernheim with George W. Cox, by that year there were an additional eight Union Churches.

From 1759 through 1797 at least seventeen more churches were founded in this area, with about half of them (eight) being union churches. The Lutheran Churches were Reformation (Heidelberg) Church in Davie County, Brick Church in Guilford County, Union Church in Rowan County, Nazareth Church in Forsyth County, Beulah (Sower's) Church and Bethany Church in Davidson County and St. Paul's Church in Alamance County, and St. Luke's Church in Davidson County.

---

[29] MORGAN, PP336-337

The other nine were all union churches. These were Daniel's Church in Lincoln County, Coldwater Church in Cabarrus County, Stoner's Church in Alamance County, Beck's Church in Davidson County, Emanuel Church in Lincolnton, Bethany (Fredericktown) Church in Davidson County, Barton (Richlands) Church in Randolph County, Salem Church in Lincoln County and Grace Church in Catawba County. We will detail here only the eight union churches.

"But while almost always devoid of pastoral leadership, these settlers early began to make provision for their own spiritual nurture and that of their families. Devout lay persons were gathering their relatives and German-speaking neighbors for worship in at least informal congregations as early as 1745, even though for many years the best they could expect by way of worship leadership was the equivalent of a lay reader, an occasional visit from a Moravian missionary, or the services of some wandering German whose pastoral credentials might not withstand close scrutiny. It seems probable that the congregations that later became known as Friedens, Gibsonville; St. John's and Zion (Organ), Salisbury; and St. John's, Concord, were already functioning congregations by 1750. In the next two decades Low's, Liberty; St. Paul's, Alamance; Reformation, Mocksville; Philadelphia, Dallas; Daniel's, Lincolnton; St. Paul's, Newton; Pilgrim, Lexington; and Cold Water, Concord, emerged as congregations."[30]

Low's, "(Lau's) Church is located in Randolph County, N. C., eighteen miles southeast from Greensboro and two miles from the Alamance battle-ground, where was fought the battle between the British and the Regulators in May, 1771.

"No early records have been preserved, but the congregation must have been organized at a very early date, probably by Nussman or Arends, who made frequent ministerial journeys into

---

[30] BOST AND NORRIS, PP24-25

that section of country. The congregation has always been Lutheran, never having united with the German Reformed, as so many of the early congregations did.

"When the first house of worship was built, how long it was used, and what was its character, nothing is known except that it was the inevitable log-house of the pioneer period.

"The second house was a frame building. Both houses stood very near the present location. The present building is a neat frame structure, with a roomy vestibule, and the pulpit between the doors as you enter the auditorium. It is 60 x 40, and has a seating capacity of five hundred.

"Just in the rear of the church is the old graveyard, where lie the earthly remains of two Lutheran ministers, Rev. Jacob Grieson and Rev. B. C. Hall.

"The congregation no doubt participated in the organization of the Synod in 1803, and took an active part in discussions and struggles growing out of the rupture that resulted in the formation of the Tennessee Synod."[31]

Notwithstanding the above quotation from Bernheim and Cox, from Welker we read:

"The first permanent ministrations of the Gospel enjoyed by these people was under the pastorate of the Rev. Samuel Suther, who preached in a small log-house built by the Reformed and Lutherans, where Low's (Lutheran) Church now stands, and about a mile south of the 'Brick Church.' The Reformed worshiped there

---

[31] BERNHEIM AND COX, P112

until during the war of the Revolution, when owing to some quarrel the door was locked, and the Reformed Church, choosing rather to suffer wrong and sacrifice their property than to persist in the use of their right at the expense of peace and quiet, withdrew. The real or ostensible cause for this violent and summary action cannot now be certainly determined; but doubtless it grew out of the question of the war itself, for while the Reformed almost to a man were patriots, the Lutherans with equal unanimity were loyalists. They at once removed to their school-house, and soon built a new and larger one to serve also for a church."[32]

Beginnings of Brick Church are conflicting in the various records available. Morgan states that the first building was in use as far back as 1765 or 1770, while Peeler puts the date at the year 1764 when the Reformed and Lutheran neighbors moved jointly to erect a log cabin at the present Low's Lutheran Church site. They worshiped together until the Revolutionary War when they separated during the pastorate of Rev. Samuel Suther when the Reformed congregation was locked out by the Lutherans. Rather than cause further trouble with their neighbors, the Reformed withdrew to the schoolhouse on the Clapp's Church grounds.[33]

A Nixon, writing in 1898, describes the hardy people of Lincoln County as a hardy people worshiping in the "Old School House Church" until 1833 wen they formally adopted the name Daniel's Church, after John Daniel Warlick and his family, founders of the church.[34]

"Next to St. Paul's in Catawba County, this [Daniel's Reformed Church] is the oldest Reformed congregation west of the Catawba River. Up to 1889, it was united with Daniel's

---

[32] WELKER, P121

[33] MORGAN, P236; PEELER P177

[34] PEELER, P200

Evangelical Lutheran Church, both congregations occupying the same house of worship, using it on alternate Sabbaths. No definite data can be given for the building of the first house of worship, but it was no doubt early in Rev. Loretz's pastorate, which began in 1786.

"The name Daniel's was given in honor of Daniel Warlick, the first of that family to settle in this section, and one of the most noted of the members and leaders of the church and community. Some years ago a document was discovered in Charlotte, among the court records of Mecklenburg County, which sets forth that this name was given by an order of the court.

"The oldest extant records of Daniel's Reformed Church date back to 1809, but the congregation is much older, for members of the Reformed Church were living in this section as early, at least, as 1750."[35]

"Coldwater Reformed Church dated from the years that immediately followed the exodus of the German Protestants from Pennsylvania to the Carolinas. The church now known as Mt. Gilead [New Gilead] is the successor of the old Coldwater Church, which had its name from a well-known stream in that region on whose banks the early German settlers of Cabarrus (then Mecklenburg) made their homes. This Coldwater Church was the oldest Reformed Church in that part of the State. No records of organization can be discovered, but most probably it may have been done by Rev. Samuel Suther, who already in 1768 was its pastor."[36]

"Coldwater Church is located near Coldwater Creek, two miles east from Concord, in Cabarrus County, N. C. It was first a German Reformed congregation, and as such dates back as far as

---

[35] WELKER, P248

[36] WELKER, PP202-203

1768, five years before Nussman and Arends came from Germany.

"About 1782 the Lutherans belonging to St. John's Church, and living in the neighborhood of Coldwater Creek, joined with the German Reformed to form a union congregation. Land for a church site was deeded to the congregation, in that year, by Adam Bowers, and Martin Phifer was made Trustee of the congregation. The house that was built was of hewn logs, and was not completed until about 1834."[37] Despite this statement by *Bernheim and Cox,* people at Coldwater Lutheran Church contest that Lutherans from St. John's organized Coldwater and remark that none of the original members were on the rolls at St. John's.

Stoner's Church in Alamance County "was first very probably a Union Reformed and Lutheran Church, with what is now St. Paul's Lutheran Church, Alamance County. It was founded not later than 1773.

"About the year 1800 the Reformed element in the congregation withdrew...and organized Stoner's Reformed Church on the site of the present cemetery..."

After a long struggle including a reorganization as "Steiner's Church" the congregation again disapeared from the rolls of the Classis of North Carolina.[38]

"Beck's is one of the old Reformed Churches in North Carolina. It has had a long and honorable history. Its first members were German settlers from the Palatinate and other sections of Europe. They brought with them their German Bibles, hymn-books

---

[37] BERNHEIM AND COX, PP103-104

[38] PEELER, PP353-354

and catechisms, some of which are still preserved as precious heirlooms in the homes of their descendants.

"The name arose from the family of Becks (Pecks) in the community. This is still a common name in the membership of this historical congregation. The meager records do not show that the church ever had any other name, though it is presumed that it had, just as the mother church of that section, Leonard's Church, was organized under the name of Pilgrim. But if there was such a name it has long since been lost sight of, and the church continues to be called 'Beck's Church.'

"The deed of the Beck's Church land bears the date of November 5, 1787,. . ."[39]

"Pilgrim Church is located four miles North of Lexington, one half mile West of the Old Greensboro Highway...There in 1753 or perhaps 1754, Pioneer Jacob Berrier and his neighbors decided should be erected a 'meeting house'." "The date when the church was organized is in question. Some claim that it occurred as early as 1754, certainly not later than 1757."[40]

Four years later, in 1757, "Lutherans came in as co-tenants, and from that time on had the use of the church and the lands. There is no record of the terms on which they were admitted."[41]

"Reformed and Lutheran brethren lived peaceably together until 1821, when an unfortunate rupture occurred in the Lutheran

---

[39] WELKER, PP103-104

[40] PEELER, P349

[41] PEELER, P350

section of the Dutch Congregation. The Lutheran Church was divided. Teo congregations resulted; one affiliating with the North Carolina Synod, and the other with the Tennessee Synod. All three groups then operated in the same building until 1903, when in the interest of peace and goodwill, an arbitrating committee was appointed to recommend an acceptable plan for the dissolution of the property...the land was sold in three tracts...Since that time the Pilgrim Reformed Congregation has been operating in the original site of the Dutch Congregation...”[42]

Emanuel's Reformed Church (the "Old White Church"), Lincolnton; "This church was in Lincolnton, in old Lincoln County of Revolutionary fame. A large part of this county was settled as early as 1745-50, when the Germans found Pennsylvania too straight for them and turned their faces to a sunnier and more fertile clime. In the vicinity of this county town were found the Hokes, Reinhardts, Summeys, Fingers, Shufords, Anthonys, Ramsaurs, Summerrows and others, who united with their Lutheran neighbors and built a church in the town of Lincolnton.

"On December 14, 1785, General Joseph Dickson entered for the citizens of Lincoln County the tract of land on which the town of Lincolnton stands, consisting of 300 acres of vacant land, and the town was laid off in lots in 1786. The same year the first court house was built and was constructed of logs. During the sessions of the court held in Lincolnton, in the old log court house, a man named Thomas Perkins, or Thomas Hawkditch, was killed by falling from one of the open windows. As there was no vacant space within the corporation for the purpose of burial, the body was taken south of the court house, and buried within a short distance of the corporation limits. When the Lutherans and

---

[42] PEELER, P351

Reformed desired to build a church, the question arose where to put it. The place where this man was buried was suggested as being central and convenient, and accordingly was selected as the site for the church and afterwards became the cemetery of the old 'White Church.'

"In the autumn of 1786 or 1787, Rev. Andrew Loretz came to Lincoln County, N. C. Here he made a home for himself four and a half miles from Lincolnton, from whence he never moved ... He was pastor of the Lincoln County Reformed Church, but he for many years itinerated over the entire territory of North and South Carolina, as far as settled by members of the Reformed Church. To him, perhaps more than any one man, the existence of the Reformed Church in North Carolina is due."[43]

"On January 10, 1788, 'Joseph Dickson, Proprietor in Trust for the citizens of Lincoln County, in consideration of ten shillings,' deeded 'two acres and sixteen poles in the South East Square of the town of Lincolnton to Christian Reinhardt, agent for the 'Dutch Presbyterians,' and Andrew Heedick, agent for the 'Dutch Lutherans,' in a part of which the Dutch Meeting House for Public Worship now stands.'"[44]

Those "Societies" had already built a house for public worship at their own expense and, not being incorporated, were desirous of their trustees acquiring the land in fee simple. That house was a one-story log building of colonial design with crude wooden furniture until 1819 when a second story was added, it was weatherboarded and ceiled. A high pulpit with stairs from either side and high-backed pews were added. The "Old White Church" was consumed by fire the night of December 23, 1893. By 1898

---

[43] COLONIAL RECORDS, VOL. VIII P747

[44] WELKER, P274

the Lutherans had built their own edifice on the property, and by 1910 the Reformeds were worshiping in New Emanuel Church in Lincolnton.[45]

"To write the history of Bethany Church is to give the history of the German people who settled in that community - a people simple in habits of life, industrious, of upright character, true devotion to the church, and strong in the faith of a Saviour's love.

"The deed conveying the property was made August 1, 1789, '... to be for the use of building a meeting-house and other religious purposes.' Frederick Miller signed the deed by making his mark.

"The first church must have been built about the time the deed was made... The first name by which the place was called was Fredericktown, in honor of Frederick Miller. Later on it was called Possumtown. And thereby hangs a tale. It is said that while the good people were at church, some one without the spirit of worship in his bosom caught several opossums, stuck their tails through a stick and left them at Frederick Miller's house; and from that time the place was known as Possumtown, which clung to it until 1861, when the new church was dedicated. No one seemed to know what name would be given the church. The dedication sermon had been preached, Rev. P. A. Long read the service of dedication, and in that dedicated the church as Bethany. The name is beautiful, and it carries our minds to the place where Jesus so often rested just outside Jerusalem."[46]

Barton Reformed Church; "The northeast corner of this county [Randolph] was peopled, as Guilford, by Germans from Pennsylvania. At an early day the Reformed and Lutherans built a

---

[45] PEELER, P215

[46] WELKER. PP172-173

union church, still known as 'Richlands.' Owing perhaps to the same causes that made the separation in the "Low" Church, the Reformed people soon moved to a house of their own, built near the village of Liberty, on the road that led from Guilford Court House to Cross Creek, or Fayetteville. . . . The deed bears date April 28, 1791."[47]

"Richland Church is located in Randolph County, four miles north from Liberty.

"Emigrants from Pennsylvania settled here between the years 1750 and 1760, and, according to the best information, organized the congregation about the year 1791, under the leadership of Rev. Christian Eberhardt Bernhardt, who came to this vicinity in 1789. The congregation was then composed of Lutherans and German Reformed, and continued thus until about the year 1802, when it became wholly Lutheran."[48]

"Salem Reformed (Union) Church, Lincoln County. The original founders of Salem Church were: John Ramsaur, Henry Ramsaur, Jacob Killian, Anthony Hallman, Henry Cressamore, Jonas Rudisill, Henry Gross, Jonas Heedick, David Carpenter and John Cline. Three of these were Reformed, namely, John Ramsaur, Henry Ramsaur and David Carpenter.

"The first church building was a house made of logs, but when built we have no means of knowing, for there are no records preserved prior to 1814. The oldest inscription found in the cemetery is that on the monument of Antoine Hes or Has, born

---

[47] WELKER, PP135-136

[48] BERNHEIM AND COX, P124

1762; died December 25, A. D. 1792."[49]

"As far as is known no Reformed Church minister preached regularly at Salem before 1849."[50] This is verification of the remarks made earlier of the unavailability of both Lutheran and Reformed ministers during the early years.

As of July 2001 Salem still serves Lutherans and United Church of Christ.

"Few congregations in the Reformed Church in North Carolina are richer in history than Grace Reformed Church [Catawba County], and few have less records from which a correct history can be written. Services were held in this community prior to the establishment of the congregation, and the tradition is that these services were held in a large double barn during the summer, and in private houses during the winter months. In the year 1796 a meeting was held in the neighborhood to consider the propriety of building a house for public worship, and on January 11, 1797, a deed for a tract of land containing a fraction over three acres was executed by Samuel E. Jarrett to John Yoder and John Huffman for the purpose of building a house of worship thereon, the consideration being eight dollars.

"The community united in erecting a log structure thirty feet long, twenty-five feet wide and two stories high. The building of a church in those days was an undertaking of great interest to the community, and it is said that the building was two years in being completed. This was built as a union church by the Reformed and

---

[49] WELKER, PP278-279

[50] PEELER, P362

Lutheran denominations, and is held as such today [1908]."[51]

    With the coming of the nineteenth century, there was less a need for union churches, for the population density and the availability of pastors had increased to a point where the individual faiths were more able to establish churches of their own. However, there were still at least fourteen more union churches created. These were Emanuel Church in Davidson County, Zion Church in Guilford County, St. John's Church in Catawba County, St. Michael's Church in Troutman, Coble's Church in Guilford County, Friendship Church in Alexander County, St. Paul's (Holshouser's) Church in Rowan County, Mt. Hope Church in Guilford County, [New] Gilead Church in Cabarrus County, Hedrick's Grove Church and Jerusalem Church in Davidson County, St. Mark's Church in Alamance County, Shiloh Church in Rowan County and St. Mark's Church in Rowan County. St. Michael's Church in Troutman was a Lutheran and Episcopal union church.

    "Emanuel Church is situated three and a half miles south of Thomasville, in Davidson County, and is one of the old churches in that section. It has always been a union church, the Lutherans sharing the property with the Reformed. The site is a fine one and easily accessible. The site was a burying ground as early as 1808 and likely also a place of worship. According to the custom of those early days a rude log church was first built, which in this instance was also used for school purposes. The place was then called 'Bowers' Meeting House.' There is no record of a congregation here prior to about 1814."[52]

---

[51] WELKER, PP264-265

[52] WELKER, P178

First known as "Bowers Meeting-House," a deed was recorded February 20, 1813 by Elizabeth Myers, daughter of John Bowers for three acres of land for five dollars to the "Elders of the Presbyterian (Reformed) and Lutheran German Churches." The proper name of the church has always been Emanuel.[53]

"Zion Church is located fourteen miles south from Greensboro, in Guilford County, N. C. It was organized about the year 1812, by Rev. Jacob Scherer, and was composed of members transferred from Lau's Church, with which it has always been in pastorate relation. At first it was a union church, composed of Lutherans and German Reformed. In 1820, when the Tennessee Synod was organized, a part of the Lutherans united with that Synod, and from then until 1845 there were three congregations worshiping in one house. Then it became wholly Lutheran, and remains so to this day, although two congregations are jointly owning the property [1908]."[54]

St. John's Church, Catawba County; "About 1812, when the first house of worship at St. Paul's gave place to the one still standing, that part of the Reformed and Lutheran congregations which lived in the bend of the Catawba River, and at an inconvenient distance, erected for themselves a commodious log building about six miles northeast of the mother church. The logs were quite large and were hauled a long distance. Hitherto many of the worshipers walked nine miles to preaching at St. Paul's."[55]

"In 1812, when St. Paul's Church located three miles

---

[53] PEELER, P208

[54] BERNHEIM AND COX, P153

[55] WELKER, P285

west of Newton, acted to erect a new sanctuary, Reformed and Lutheran members living in the 'bend of Catawba River' two miles Northeast of Conover, withdrew from the mother church, in the interest of convenience, and erected one of their own in the St. John's community."[56]

"St. Michael's Church is located in the town of Troutman, in Iredell County, N. C., on the A. T. and O. R. R., about six miles from Statesville.

"The congregation was organized in 1815, by Rev. R. J. Miller, and was admitted to Synod in October of the same year, under the name of "New Pearth." The organization was effected in "Cambridge Associate Presbyterian Church," about two miles south from the present location, where the first communion was had on August 27th, 1815. The congregation continued to worship there until about the year 1823, when a Mr. Daniel Walcher donated land for a church site about one and one-quarter miles southwest from where Troutman's now is. The land was given to the Lutherans and Episcopalians jointly, and upon it they erected a union house of worship, made of logs, about 36 x 25. For several years both denominations worshiped in this house, then the Episcopalians voluntarily withdrew and erected a church of their own a few miles distant. The date of this movement is not known, but persons who have been reared in the neighborhood, and who are now fifty years old, have never heard an Episcopal clergyman preach there.

"About the year 1850 the house was considerably enlarged and improved, and the congregation continued to worship in it until it had erected the present building. The corner-stone was laid

---

[56] PEELER, P422

August 19th, 1886, and the dedicatory services were held August 14th, 1892, by the pastor, Rev. D. W. Michael, assisted by Rev. Prof. J. D. Shirey, D. D. It is a handsome frame building, 60 x 36, with recess, council-rooms, etc. . . .

"The congregation, in the past, has been very strong; the present membership is two hundred and twelve. [1902]"[57]

Coble's Church, Guilford County. Information on this church comes from four references, *Historic Sketch of the Reformed Church in North Carolina, History of the Evangelical Lutheran Synod and Ministerium of North Carolina, All One Body: The Story of the North Carolina Lutheran Synod, 1803-1993,* and *A Story of the Southern Synod of the Evangelical and Reformed Church* is very limited. From the first source, we find on September 26, 1830, Coble's congregation was represented at the first meeting to organize the North Carolina Classis in Hagerstown, Md.[58], then in 1839 the meeting of the Classis was held at Coble's Church in Guilford County.[59] The Mt. Hope Church of Guilford County had members coming from Coble's Church (a union of Lutherans and Reformed) about 1847 or 1848. *Bernheim and Cox* had no mention of Coble's. In 1877, according to *Bost and Norris,* the 1877 Tennessee Synod convention was held at Coble's. According to the last-mentioned source, the congregation was in existence as early as 1812 and bore the name Coble's Church in deference to the large number of the Coble clan which worshiped there.[60] Rev. Michael Leonard Fox, M. D.

---

[57] BERNHEIM AND COX, PP144-145

[58] WELKER, P51

[59] WELKER, P68

[60] PEELER, P310

served Coble's as stated supply over his 21-year ministry that was limited to accepting a call only from one church because of his extended medical practice, according to Bost and Norris.[61]

"It was a union church, used jointly by Reformed and Lutheran families until 1847. At that time the Reformed element withdrew and organized Mt. Hope Church in Guilford County."[62]

"The Reformed Church in North Carolina has failed to enter many communities in which there was a Reformed constituency, and in some cases after entering a community and establishing congregations has suffered these organizations to disband for want of pastoral care. This was the case in Caldwell, now Alexander County. It is evident that many of the early settlers in this county were adherents to the Reformed and Lutheran Churches. Rev. A. L. Crouse (Lutheran) in his Historical Sketches says: 'A large proportion, if not a majority, of the Germans who settled in Alexander County belonged to what was then the German Reformed Church. These were the Richards, Hermans, Rowes, Benfields, Kellers, Prices and some say the Wittenbergers.' Some of these at least must have crossed the Catawba River and worshiped with the congregations in Catawba County. The Lutherans established Friendship Church in the year 1833 and it is highly probable that the Reformed people held occasional services at this place. The Reformed people organized a congregation in this county in the year 1844, but it has been difficult to obtain much correct information concerning it. The following found on the first page of a little book belonging to the late Rev. Jeremiah Ingold, D.D., is about all the record that we have been enabled to find relating to this congregation:

---

[61] WELKER, PP 51, 68, 101, 113, 136; BOST AND NORRIS, PP 180, 375

[62] PEELER, P 444

44

"ECCLESIASTICAL MEMORANDUM.

"'Commencing on the third Sabbath in May, 1844. I was ordained on the 4th of April at the Brick Church, Guilford County. Took charge of the congregation at Friendship, Caldwell County. Preached my introductory sermon on the 3d Sunday of May. The congregation had been organized about two months previous by Rev. J. H. Crawford.'"[63]

"The Mt. Hope [not the Mt. Hope below] congregation of the Guilford Charge was organized by the Rev. G. W. Welker, D.D., with members who came from Coble's Church, a union Lutheran and Reformed Church, about 1847 or 1848. Dr. Welker had preached on Sunday evenings at Neece's School House for some time near where the church was afterwards built. Then a brush arbor was built, which soon gave way to a better one covered with boards. The first church, a brick building, was erected in 1851."[64]

At Friendship Church Reformed and Lutheran Brethren evidently worshiped together in a "Log Meeting House" which provided galleries for the use of slaves during worship. The Reformed members laid a cornerstone for their own church in September 1844, but it was never completed. The only remaining evidence of that church is a small cemetery of 24 unmarked grave headstones.[65]

"St. Paul's congregation, also known as Holshouser's

---

[63] WELKER, PP310-311

[64] WELKER, P136

[65] PEELER, P447

Church, was organized in March, 1850, by the Rev. John Lantz, with seventeen members: . . . St. Paul's was situated about four miles from Salisbury near the New Concord Road in the neighborhood of Holshouser's Mill, now known as the old Heilig Mill. St. Paul's was originally built as a union church by the members of the Reformed and Lutheran Churches. Andrew Holshouser, member of the Reformed Church, gave the land on which the church was built. But by some means the Lutherans came into possession while the church was still incomplete, for after the Reformed congregation was organized the Lutherans proposed that if the Reformed would assist in finishing the church they should have an interest in the property. But it seems that the Reformed, having obtained an interest in the property, lost it through a mistranslation of the German word 'Reformirte,' which was rendered into English by the word 'Presbyterian.'

"In November, 1865, the Classis of North Carolina authorized the Rev. Thornton Butler to disband the congregation at St. Paul's and organize at a point about seven miles from Salisbury, on the 'New Concord Road.'

"In the year 1866 a beautiful brick church sixty by forty feet was erected. The brick were made by the members of the congregation. Before and during the erection of the building services were held in the grove. On the 14th of January, 1866, the congregation was organized under a new name, Mt. Hope Reformed Church."[66]

Slightly conflicting the above is information from *Bernheim and Cox*, particularly in the organizational date, herewith submitted:

---

[66] WELKER, PP226-227

"St. Paul's Church, Rowan County, N. C., is located five miles south from Salisbury. It was originally known as "Holshouser's Church," so named because the land was given by Andrew Holshouser, near where was the Holshouser's Mill, now known as the Heilig Mill. Mr. Holshouser was a member of the German Reformed Church, and the congregation was a union congregation. It was organized about the year 1835. The first mention of it is in the Minutes of the Synod of 1837. In 1866 it became wholly Lutheran, the German Reformed establishing what is now known as 'Mt. Hope Church.'"[67]

And in Peeler, we note: "Tradition relates that the congregation was organized March 30, 1830...the organizer was Rev. John Lantz. Rev. Samuel Rothrock, the first regular minister to the Lutheran element in the community, who served there beginning 1835, relates in his diary that he held services regularly once a month at Holshouser's Church, and that he attended the wedding there of Rev. John Lantz to Miss Nancy Fraley April 23, 1845."[68]

From the above, it is apparent that the information of Welker could be misconstrued. Peeler seems to make it very clear that St. Paul's Church, four and a half miles south of Salisbury, originally known as Holshouser's was organized in 1832.[69] St. Paul's German Reformed Church was founded March 1850 by John Lantz with seventeen people on the original roll. This St. Paul's was never a union church.[70]

---

[67] BERNHEIM AND COX, P132

[68] PEELER, P325

[69] PEELER, P325

[70] PEELER, P326

New Gilead Reformed Church, Cabarrus County. See Coldwater Church, previously discussed.

"The original members of Hedrick's Grove were transferred mainly from Beck's. The congregation was organized the first Sunday in May, 1891, with forty-one members.

"This church [Jerusalem] is in the southern part of Davidson County, distant some twelve or fourteen miles south-east of Lexington. The congregation was organized by Rev. Thornton Butler in 1858 for the convenience of the members of Beck's Church who were living too far from their place of worship. It is a union church and forms a part of the Lower Davidson Charge. It has never had a large membership, but has been active in good works."[71]

"...This place became a preaching point as early as 1852, when Rev. Thornton Butler, a German Reformed Church minister, held services in the community under an apple tree...on August 28, 1856 Levi Beck deeded a tract of land...A Lutheran Church was organized in 1856 and it appears that in the latter part of 1857, a Reformed Church was established, Rev. Thornton Butler being the organizer..."[72]

"St. Mark's Reformed Church is located one and one-fourth miles south of Elon College in Alamance County. The late Rev. G. W. Wackier [Welker], D.D., in his notes on the origin of this congregation says that it was organized at Frieden's, about nine miles northwest of the Brick Church soon after the Brick Church was organized, and probably by the same minister who organized

---

[71] WELKER, P185

[72] PEELER, P331

48

the Brick Church. Frieden's was a union Reformed and Lutheran Church and was located about two miles northwest of Gibsonville. It was also known as "Schumaker's Church." The Reformed families in this vicinity were the Weitzells, Wyricks, Straders, DeWalds and others, who here were wont to worship until the congregation by neglect was under the ministry of Rev. Crawford suffered to disintegrate. However, on the 13th of January, 1855, under the ministry of Rev. G. W. Welker, this congregation was re-organized.

"For the convenience of its members in 1857 the Reformed congregation withdrew and held services under a brush arbor two miles southeast of Gibsonville near Boon's Station on the old stage road leading from Salisbury to Hillsboro. In 1862 the present building [1908] was erected about one-half mile south of the arbor. This is a frame structure about 40 by 60 feet. As will be seen from the date it was built in war times. Many of the residents in the community can well remember when it was built. They say it was enclosed and the floor laid and used in this way for a long time before it was plastered."[73]

"The congregation was known as 'Shoemaker's' and operated peacefully as a union church with the Lutheran segment of that community for many years."[74]

"Shiloh Reformed Church was organized March 19, 1871, by the Rev. J. C. Denny, pastor of the East Rowan Charge, which at that time consisted of Lower Stone, Bear Creek and Mt. Hope. Seventeen persons entered into the organization. . . Mt. Hope was then separated from the East Rowan Charge and joined with Shiloh

---

[73] WELKER, PP144-145

[74] PEELER, P388

to constitute the Central Rowan Charge. For some time previous to the organization services had been held in an old log school-house by Rev. Denny and P. M. Trexler, a student for the ministry. The organization was effected for the convenience of the Reformed people living in Salisbury and its vicinity, who were at too great a distance from Mt. Hope or Lower Stone to make it convenient for them to worship at either place. The church was built during the fall and winter preceding the organization by the members, with F. M. Holshouser and Lawson Fisher as foremen. About two miles southwest of the location of the new church stood an old frame church building, owned by the Methodists, and called Shiloh; but owing to want of members and lack of interest the congregation had passed out of existence. This building was purchased for a small sum, and as much of it as could be profitably used was wrought into the new structure. For this reason, and because some of the few Methodists remaining cast in their lot with the Reformed, the new church fell heir to the name of the defunct Methodist organization, and was called Shiloh. The cost of this building and the date of its dedication are not known. . . Student P. M. Trexler, having been licensed by the Classis on June 2, 1871. served jointly with Rev. Denny the new congregation until Sunday, September 17, 1871, when the former was ordained and installed as pastor. . . On the Saturday preceding, immediately after the preparatory services, a meeting of the Joint Consistories of the Rowan Charges was held, at which time were adopted and signed the famous "Shiloh Resolutions," which had been drawn up by Rev. Denny. An interesting special meeting of Classis was held in this church in December, 1871, to consider the "Shiloh Resolutions," and also an overture from the Dutch Reformed Church inviting North Carolina Classis to unite with that body. . .

". . .In November, 1877, some of the members proposed to their pastor that they hold a week or ten days revival service. Rev.

50

Denny consented. At this time the Methodists of the Western District of the North Carolina Conference were holding their annual sessions at Salisbury. The meeting at Shiloh had continued but a few days when it was suggested that application be made to the Methodist Conference for preachers to help carry on the meeting. The request of course was gladly and promptly granted, and some of their best men were sent out each day, two at a time. The meeting grew daily in interest, the attendance being very great. As a consequence, the power and influence of the Methodist preachers grew every day, until the building of a Methodist Church began to be agitated; in a few days more it was suggested that Shiloh Reformed congregation go over to the Methodist Church. This movement came very near taking the whole Reformed congregation at one sweep into the Methodist Church. Every one seemed to be wrought up to a high tension along this line; but just in time, under the Providence of God, some of the good old Reformed Church members began to get upon their feet and to think seriously about what was taking place. Those who saved the day for the Reformed Church by refusing to surrender the property were John Wilson Fisher, Daniel M. Klutts, F. Monroe Holshouser and Crawford Peeler. As a result of this disaffection fully one-half of the membership of Shiloh was swept into the Methodist Church. Much bitter feeling and strife was engendered, which did not finally disappear until the lapse of five or six years. The pastor, Rev. Denny, having sorely compromised himself in the whole sad affair, was regarded as the one most to blame. The Classis cited him to trial to answer for his conduct, but fearing the consequences he left the Reformed Church, made application to and was received as a minister into the Baptist Church. Thus ended a disagreeable experience in the history of this congregation whose name means peace. Rev. Denny was succeeded by Rev. John Ingle, who took charge January 1, 1878, and closed his pastorate January 1, 1883...

"On August 26, 1898, a meeting was held at Faith, Rowan County, to consider the advisability of securing the removal of Shiloh Reformed Church to that place. Faith at that time was a small village built along the old Charleston Road, three miles south of Shiloh Church, and contained about two hundred inhabitants, nearly all of whom were members of the Lutheran and Reformed Churches, although there was no church in the village. For some time previous to the above date a union Sunday School had been conducted in the public school building, and a prosperous Young Men's Christian Association had been formed. At this meeting in August, 1898, after a thorough discussion it was ordered that a petition be placed in the hands of D. A. Wiley (Lutheran) to secure the signature of all persons desiring to enter the organization to report on the 2d of September, 1898. The proposition had been made that the Lutherans join with the Reformed at Shiloh and at Faith in a union church at the latter place, hence the appointment of D. A. Wiley to circulate the petition. On the second of September, 1898, a number of persons met according to adjournment. D. A. Wiley failed to appear. The reason for this failure of Wiley to appear was owing to the fact that the Lutherans, fortunately for both themselves and the Reformed, concluded that the necessity for union churches no longer existed, and resolved to organize a church of their own. Another petition was placed in the hands of John A. Peeler. On September 4, 1898, the petition from the Reformed members at Faith was presented to the Shiloh congregation, and on the seventh of September Shiloh congregation met and decided that it did not see its way clear at that time to move its place of worship to Faith. . . In the fall of 1899 the old Shiloh church building was sold to Wesley Brown, one of the members, for seventy-five dollars. The building was transferred to Granite Quarry and converted into a store building. Shiloh congregation, though now located at Faith, still holds the original tract of land [1908], including cemetery, which is cared for by the members. The congregation also owns a cemetery in Faith."[75][76]

---

[75] WELKER, PP219-225

[76] PEELER, PP358-359: THE FAMOUS "SHILOH RESOLUTIONS"

Thankfully we have had the unceasing efforts of the early pioneers such as Christian Theus, Samuel Suther, Adolph Nussman, Gottfried Arends, and a host of others in forming these Unions. We have the written records from G. D. Bernheim, George W. Cox, Raymond Bost, Jeff Norris, Carl Hammer, Frank Bostian, Tom and Reedy Moose, my father, Bernard Cruse, Sr., William Saunders, Donald Phillips, Jacob Morgan, Bachman S. Brown, Jr., John Hall, and many others whose untiring labors have helped preserve records of these unions. Unfortunately our predecessors were too busy making history and striving to simultaneously earn their living to record it properly. In many cases their written records were lost due to wars, fires and other natural causes. For further information this writer urges the reader to consult the books listed in "Sources," readily available in many libraries and church archives.

As mentioned earlier, as the twentieth century brought forth population growth and easier transportation and communication, need for union churches almost ended and the mighty churches that have been formed since have been created and sustained by their own organizations. Today (July 2001) there is only one union church of Lutheran and United Church of Christ still on the rolls of the North Carolina Synod - Evangelical Lutheran Church in America and the Western North Carolina Association of the Southern Conference of the United Church of Christ. That is Salem Church in Lincolnton first organized in 1792. Let us never forget them or the others who eventually formed congregations within their own faith.

Epilogue

Sadly, not every one of the Lutheran and Reformed Union Churches survived as union churches or as individual congregations. Reasons were varied; some merged into other churches, some reorganized and some were simply discontinued because of population removals or other reasons.

There was a Lutheran and Reformed union in Gaston County near Paysewer's Mill which burned during the Revolutionary War and of which no records are available.[77]

In Catawba County, about three miles south of the present St. James Lutheran Church and about the same distance southeast of Newton is an old, large overgrown cemetery. Nearby once stood "Old Haas" or Haas Church. The *History of Catawba County* edited by Charles J. Preslar, Jr. states that "the Church was used by both Lutheran and Reformed members until 1845, when the Reformed members withdrew and built a church of their own in Newton." The *History of the Lutheran Church in North Carolina* makes the same assertion, giving the date of the Reformed withdrawal as 1852. The Lutherans remained until 1867 when the Lutherans founded St. James Lutheran Church about one mile northwest. Tradition has it that Reformed people continued using it until the organization of Memorial Reformed Church in Maiden.

---

[77] CLAPP, P245

Appendix A

Some of the North Carolina Union Churches

Second Creek (Hickory Church), parent of	
Organ Lutheran and Grace (Lowerstone) UCC	1745
Barren (Bear) Creek, parent of	
Bear Creek UCC, St. John Lutheran and New Bethel Lutheran	1745
Friedens (Schumaker's) Church, Gibsonville	175-
Low's Church, Liberty, Guilford County, see also Brick Church	175-
Shiloh Church, Forsyth County (Moravians)	early
Savitz's, parent of	
Mt. Zion UCC, Lutheran Chapel Lutheran, Mt. Moriah Lutheran	1755
Pilgrim Church (Leonard's), Davidson County	1757
St. Paul's Church, Catawba County	1759
Brick (Clapp's) Church. Alamance County	1764
Dutchman's Creek (Heidelberg, later Reformation), Mocksville	before 1766
Daniel's Church, Lincoln County parent of	
Daniel's Lutheran, Daniel UCC	1767
Cold Water Church, Cabarrus County	
parent of Coldwater Lutheran, Mt. [New] Gilead UCC	1768
Stoner's Church, Alamance County	before 1773
Beck's Church, Davidson County	1787
Beulah (Sower's) Church, Davidson County	before 1788
Emanuel Church (The Old White Church), Lincolnton	1788
Bethany Church (Fredericktown), Davidson County	1789
Barton (Richlands) Church, Randolph County	1791
Salem Church, Lincoln County	1792
Grace Church, Catawba County	1797
Emanuel Church, Davidson County	1808
Zion Lutheran Church, Guilford County	1812
St. John's Church, Catawba County	1812
St. Michael Lutheran Church, Troutman (Episcopal)	1815
Coble's Church, Guilford County	Uncertain
Friendship Church, Alexander County	1833
St. Paul's Lutheran Church, Rowan County	1835
Mt. Hope Church, Guilford County	1847
St. Paul's (Holshouser's) Church, Rowan County	1850
[New] Gilead Church, Cabarrus County, see Cold Water	1851
St. Mark's Church, Alamance County	1855
Jerusalem Church, Davidson County	1858
Shiloh Church, Rowan County	1871
Hedrick's Grove, Davidson County	1891
St. Mark's (Lutheran) Church, Rowan County	1894

Der Herr's Betener

(The Lord's Prayer)

Lutheran

Vater Unser, der du bist im himmel
Geheiliget werde Dein Name
Dein Reich komme
Dein Wille geschehe, wie im Himmel, also
      auch auf Erden
Unser Täglich Brot gib uns heute
Und vergib uns unsre Schuld als wir vergeben
      unsern Schuldigern
Und führe uns nic; in Versuchung
Söndern erlöse uns von dem Uebel
Den Dein ist das Reich, und die Kraft, und die
      Herrlichkeit, in Ewigkeit.
             Amen

Reformed

Unser Vater in dem Himmel
Dein Name werde geheiliget
Dein Reich komme. Dein Wille geische auf
      Erden, wie im Himmel.
Unser taglich Brod gieb uns heute.
Und vergieb uns unsere Schulden, wir wir
      unsern Schuldigern vergeben.
Und führe uns nicht in Versuchung,
Söndern erlose uns von dem Uebel.
Denn Dein is das Reich, und die Kraft, und
      de Herrlichkeit, in Ewigkeit.
             Amen

APPENDIX C

Sources

Bear Creek: *Dutch Buffalo Creek Meeting House, 1745-1806* by Frank K. Bostian and Bernard W. Cruse, LL. B. and *Bethel Bear Creek United Church of Christ, 1806-1974*, by Thomas L. Moose and Reedy Jordan Moose, 1974.

Bernheim and Cox: *The History of the Evangelical Lutheran Synod and Ministerium of North Carolina*, by G. D. Bernheim, D. D., and George H. Cox, D. D., 1902.

Bost and Norris: *All One Body: The Story of the North Carolina Lutheran Synod, 1803-1993*, Raymond M. Bost and Jeff L. Norris, 1994

Clapp, Jacob C.:   *Historic Sketch of the Reformed Church in North Carolina*, 1908

Colonial Records: *The Colonial Records of North Carolina*, Collected and Edited by William L. Saunders, Secretary of State, 1886

Hammer: *Rhinelanders on the Yadkin*, by Carl Hammer, Jr., M.A., Ph.D., 1943.

Lutheran Chapel: *History of Lutheran Chapel Church Since 1780*, Rev. Donald M. Phillips, undated, Ca 1984.

Morgan: *History of the Lutheran Church in North Carolina*, Edited by Jacob L. Morgan, D. D., Bachman S. Brown, Jr., D. D. and John Hall, D. D., 1953.

Peeler: *A Story of the Southern Synod of the Evangelical and Reformed Church*, Banks J. Peeler, D.D. 1968.

Welker: *Historic Sketch of the Reformed Church in North Carolina*, by a Board of Editors under the Classis of North Carolina with an Introduction by the Late Geo. Wm. Welker, D.D., 1908.

INDEX

NCR

2/03